DEPARTMENT OF THE NAVY
HEADQUARTERS UNITED STATES MARINE CORPS
3000 MARINE CORPS PENTAGON
WASHINGTON, DC 20350-3000

MARINE CORPS DIVING POLICY AND PROGRAM ADMINISTRATION

DEPARTMENT OF THE NAVY
HEADQUARTERS UNITED STATES MARINE CORPS
3000 MARINE CORPS PENTAGON
WASHINGTON, DC 20350-3000

MCO 3150.4
PP&O (POG)
4 May 2009

MARINE CORPS ORDER 3150.4

From: Commandant of the Marine Corps
To: Distribution List

Subj: MARINE CORPS DIVING POLICY AND PROGRAM ADMINISTRATION

Ref: (a) DOD Instruction 3224.04, "Single Manager Responsibility
           for Joint Service Military Diving Technology and Training (MDT&T),"
           May 23, 2008
       (b) DOD Directive 5000.01, "The Defense Acquisition System," May 12,
           2003
       (c) DOD Instruction 5000.02, "Operation of the Defense Acquisition
           System," December 8, 2008
       (d) MCO 1553.1B
       (e) MCO 1553.2A
       (f) MCO P5102.1B
       (g) OPNAVINST 5100.19E
       (h) NAVSEA SS521-AG-PRO-010 Rev 6
       (i) MCO 3500.27B
       (j) MCO 3900.15B
       (k) OPNAVINST 5450.180D
       (l) MCO 1200.17
       (m) NAVPERS 18068F
       (n) MCO 5311.1D
       (o) MCO P1000.6G
       (p) MCO P1020.34G
       (q) OPNAVINST 3150.27B
       (r) NAVSEAINST 3150.1A
       (s) SECNAV M-5210.1
       (t) NAVMED P-117
       (u) DOD 7000.14-R, "Department of Defense Financial Management
           Regulations (FMRS)," Dates Vary by Volume
       (v) MILPERSMAN 1220-260
       (w) MCO P3500.73
       (x) NAVSEAINST 4790.8B
       (y) OSHA Instruction CPL 02-00-143, "Commercial Diving Operations,"
           August 11, 2006
       (z) NAVSEA 10560 Series 00C/3112
       (aa) TI-10560-14, Maintenance and Accountability for USMC Dive
            Lockers (NOTAL)

Encl: (1) Marine Corps Diving Policy and Program Administration Manual

1. Situation. Department of Defense (DOD) executive agents (EA) establish
policy that guides the conduct and administration of individual Service
diving programs, per references (a) through (aa). Reference (a) assigns the
Assistant Secretary of Defense for Special Operations and Low-Intensity
Conflict, Department of the Navy as the DOD Diving Proponent. Additionally,

reference (a) assigns the Secretary of the Navy as the DOD Executive Agent (EA) for MDT&T. This Order establishes policy and procedural guidance for the administration of Marine Corps diving programs and takes precedence where Marine Corps equipment and doctrine are not addressed or supported by DOD EA policy, procedure and/or doctrine. All Marine Corps diving programs will be administered in compliance with this Order.

2. <u>Cancellation</u>. MCO 3500.20B.

3. <u>Mission</u>. The Marine Corps diving program supports the development and maintenance of required warfighting capabilities. Policies and procedures described herein are intended to maximize unit and individual combat effectiveness, service inter-operability, accountability and safety.

4. <u>Execution</u>

    a. <u>Commander's Intent and Concept of Operations</u>

        (1) <u>Commander's Intent</u>

            (a) All cognizant Commanders and Officers-in-Charge of Marine Corps units performing diving operations will conduct diving operations and training per this Order and other applicable directives. This Order is applicable to both the Active and Reserve Components of the USMC.

            (b) This Order is applicable to all DOD civilian and military personnel assigned to Marine Corps units and activities. When other Service or Component directives conflict with this Order, the Marine Component commander will determine which Order takes precedence.

            (c) This Order establishes the Deputy Commandant for Plans, Policies and Operations (DC, PP&O) as the Marine Corps Diving Proponent.

        (2) <u>Concept of Operations</u>. The Marine Corps develops and maintains diving capabilities to meet valid operational requirements, as indicated in CMC-approved unit mission statements and by appropriately coded billets on unit Tables of Organization (T/Os). Details of this policy, to include exceptions, are found in the enclosure to this Order.

    b. <u>Subordinate Element Missions</u>

        (1) <u>DC, PP&O (POG) shall</u>:

            (a) Serve as the USMC Diving Proponent, functional expert and supervisor in all matters related to diving per enclosure (1) of this Order.

            (b) Conduct an annual validation of all diving billets and provide applicable Diving Duty Special Pay budget input to DC, M&RA (MPP) to coincide with budget cycle submissions.

            (c) Validate all new diving requirements for USMC units and billets as a function of the Total Force Structure process prior to final approval by DC, CD&I.

            (d) Prior to initial fielding of new USMC maritime craft, coordinate DOD proponent validation and approval of craft-specific diving procedures.

(2) <u>DC, CD&I shall</u>:

(a) In conjunction with DC PP&O (POG), serve as the user representative for all diving equipment related issues, ensuring current diving equipment deficiencies are corrected and desired diving capabilities support Marine Corps required operational capabilities.

(b) Take all actions necessary to support equipment requirements for diving capabilities, per references (b) and (c).

(c) In coordination with Marine Corps Systems Command (MARCORSYSCOM), Infantry Weapons Systems, Raids and Amphibious Reconnaissance (IWS/R), maintain inter-service liaison to ensure equipment interoperability and facilitate requirement development through appropriate supporting documentation to support diving operations.

(d) Participate in all diving-related Integrated Process Action Teams (IPTs) to identify and resolve logistics issues per chapter 2, enclosure (1) of this Order.

(e) Maintain current and future T/Os and Tables of Equipment (T/Es), with mission statements, for all units with valid diving requirements.

(f) Maintain current and planned T/E allowances within the Total Force Structure Management System for all units with valid diving requirements.

(g) Publish timely updates to any T/O and T/E changes approved to units with valid diving requirements.

(3) <u>CG, Training Command (C461TP) shall</u>:

(a) Conduct an annual validation of all Marine Corps diving related formal school requirements via the Training Input Plan (TIP) process, per reference (d), and provide input and requirements to other services as required.

(b) Manage the assignment of diving related formal school quotas via the Student Registrar Module of the Marine Corps Training Information Management System (MCTIMS) per chapter 8 of the enclosure to this Order.

(c) Evaluate the applicability and effectiveness of current and proposed USMC diving training programs, per reference (e).

(d) Establish individual training standards for diving and incorporate as appropriate into associated training and readiness (T&R) manuals.

(e) Participate in all diving-related IPTs to identify and resolve training issues per chapter 2 of enclosure (1) of this Order.

(f) Develop, train and maintain Programs of Instruction (POI) for USMC-unique diving equipment as required.

(g) Consult and collaborate closely with IWS/R diving and amphibious program officers in the development of manpower and training plans for diving and other amphibious/maritime equipment in RDT&E.

(h) Participate in the USMC Diving Capabilities Conference per chapter 3 of the enclosure to this Order.

(4) <u>Commanding General, Marine Corps Systems Command (IWS/R) shall</u>:

(a) Coordinate and manage all diving-related equipment research, development and acquisition as identified by DC, CD&I and validated by DC, PP&O (POG). This includes both meeting current and emerging requirements, as well as leveraging technology to develop next-generation diving equipment.

(b) Provide Marine Corps-wide coordination and standardization of all approved and fielded diving-related systems and equipment.

(c) Serve as the Marine Corps sponsor for diving equipment, responsible for developing and refining applicable technical and procedural techniques specific to diving-related equipment, as well as monitoring /enforcing applicable safety procedures for that equipment.

(d) Provide assistance to DC, PP&O (POG) and CG TECOM (C461) with regard to diving safety, procedures, and techniques as requested.

(e) Participate in the USMC Diving Capabilities Conference per chapter 3 of the enclosure to this Order.

(f) Participate in all diving-related IPTs to identify and resolve technical, systemic and/or programmatic issues per chapter 2 of enclosure (1) of this Order.

(5) <u>Request that Commander, Naval Safety Center (Code 37), per reference (q)</u>:

(a) Advise DC PP&O (POG), DC I&L (LPC), DC CD&I, and CG, TECOM on safety matters pertaining to diving procedures and techniques.

(b) Investigate, evaluate and maintain records on all diving-related mishaps involving Marine Corps personnel and/or equipment per references (f) and (g). Ensure compliance with reference (h), and report all violations to DC, PP&O (POG).

(c) Maintain a data repository for all military dives and mishap reports. Analyze data for trends, and distribute statistics via Diving Safety Lines on a semi-annual basis, at a minimum.

(d) Participate in the USMC Diving Capabilities Conference per chapter 3 of the enclosure to this Order.

(e) Conduct safety inspections on all Marine Corps units with a diving capability at least once every 2 years. Conduct safety surveys or assist visits as requested by units or by DC, PP&O (POG).

(f) Participate in all diving-related IPTs to identify and resolve safety issues per chapter 2 of enclosure (1) of this Order.

(g) Publish and maintain a listing of all current publications pertinent to diving operations, training and maintenance.

(h) Evaluate Operational Testing (OT) and Developmental Testing (DT) of diving procedures for USN and USMC maritime craft in RDT&E.

(i) Upon completion of OT and DT of diving procedures for USN and USMC maritime craft in RDT&E, issue a Safety Confirmation to DC, PP&O (POG) certifying the accepted procedures as safe and reliable for DOD use.

(6) Marine Corps commanders/officers-in-charge of formal training units/activities shall:

(a) Administer, manage and oversee formal courses of instruction, per reference (e).

(b) Ensure all diving training and operations are conducted, per reference (i). In situations where proponent operational risk management (ORM) procedures have not adequately mitigated identified risks, report discrepancies and possible safety issues to DC, PP&O (POG).

(c) Ensure diving operations are conducted and supervised by a current Dive Supervisor trained on the type of equipment used for each training evolution.

(d) Ensure all instructor and student certification, recertification and refresher training is conducted and documented per the enclosure to this Order.

(7) Unit commanders shall:

(a) Ensure and enforce compliance with this Order and all other applicable directives within their purview.

(b) Ensure currency and qualification of all divers and Dive Supervisors and support personnel per the enclosure to this Order.

(c) Ensure certification, recertification and refresher training is conducted and documented as required per the enclosure to this Order.

(d) Ensure proper maintenance, inspection, security and storage of all diving-related equipment per this order, applicable references and equipment technical manuals per the enclosure to this Order.

(e) Develop and maintain a unit Standard Operating Procedure (SOP) for diving operations, addressing specific areas not addressed in current directives or doctrinal publications.

5. Administration and Logistics

    a. Exceptions to Policy. Requests to waive or permanently change any portion of this Order will be submitted via the first O-5 in the chain of command to DC, PP&O (POG) per chapter 5, enclosure (1) of this Order.

    b. Definitions. For the purposes of this Order, the following phrases or terms apply:

(1) <u>Marine Corps Personnel</u>. This phrase refers to all active, reserve and civilian employed USMC personnel, USMC contractors and any DOD uniformed military personnel assigned to Marine Corps units.

(2) <u>Marine Corps Diving Operations and Training</u>. This phrase refers to diving operations and training conducted under cognizance of a Marine Corps commander or officer-in-charge of a Marine Corps unit or activity.

(3) <u>Dive</u>. This term refers to the physical action of personnel performing a directed task as a function of diving operations or training while underwater and breathing from a compressed medium such as air, oxygen or mixed gases.

(4) <u>USMC-Approved Formal Course(s) of Instruction</u>. This phrase refers to courses of instruction listed in the Marine Corps Training Information Management System (MCTIMS) Course Catalog.

(5) <u>Qualified</u>. This term refers to divers and diving supervisors who have successfully completed appropriate qualification training and maintain diving proficiency such as to remain eligible for Diving Duty Special Pay (DDSP).

(6) <u>Current</u>. This term refers to qualified divers and diving supervisors who maintain proficiency such as not to require dive refresher training.

6. <u>Command and Signal</u>

   a. <u>Command</u>. This Order is applicable to the Marine Corps Total Force.

   b. <u>Signal</u>. This Order is effective the date signed.

J. F. DUNFORD, JR.
Deputy Commandant for
Plans, Policies and Operations

DISTRIBUTION: PCN 10203188300

LOCATOR SHEET

Subj: MARINE CORPS DIVING POLICY AND PROGRAM ADMINISTRATION PROCEDURAL
      MANUAL

Location: _____
           (Indicate the location(s) of the copy(ies) of this Order.)

RECORD OF CHANGES

Log completed change action as indicated.

Change Number	Date of Change	Date Entered	Signature of Person Incorporating Change

Enclosure (1)

TABLE OF CONTENTS

TABLE OF CONTENTS

TABLE OF CONTENTS

Chapter 1

Proponency

1. General. This chapter provides detailed information on the authority, definition and scope of proponency of Marine Corps diving programs.

2. Authority. Reference (a) designates the United States Navy as the EA for military diving operations. This Order establishes DC, PP&O (POG) as the proponent for all USMC diving.

3. Definition. As proponent for USMC diving, DC, PP&O (POG) is responsible for coordination of all aspects of the development, sustainment, and maintenance of that capability and is vested with the authority to organize and direct appropriate actions to accomplish such objectives.

4. Scope. Tasks unique to individual proponents are identified in paragraph 4b of this chapter. Common tasks associated with USMC diving proponency include, but are not limited to the following:

a. Advocacy

    (1) Serve in the role of lead advocate in the development of USMC diving capabilities, per reference (j).

    (2) Serve in the role of diving advocates in the development of maritime capabilities, per reference (j).

    (3) Conduct inter-service coordination and liaison for Marine Corps diving operations and training.

    (4) Establish, direct, enforce and monitor Marine Corps integrated process teams (IPTs) to identify and resolve issues related to diving capabilities, operations, training and equipment.

    (5) Sponsor the USMC Diving Capabilities Conference per chapter 3 of this Order.

    (6) Serve in the role of Marine Corps diving proponent in all matters associated with DOD executive agents.

b. Policy

    (1) Establish, enforce and monitor policy to ensure Marine Corps-wide applicability and compliance.

    (2) Serve as the sole authority to waive Marine Corps diving policy.

    (3) Initiate Marine Corps-wide corrective/preventative action pertaining to USMC diving as required.

c. Training. Monitor and enforce proper usage of seats to formal diving courses of instruction per chapter 8 of this Order.

Chapter 2

Capability Development

1. General. This chapter outlines requirements pertaining to the development of USMC diving and maritime capabilities.

2. Diving Capability Development. USMC diving capabilities will be developed to meet valid and approved operational requirements per reference (j).

3. Integrated Process Action Teams (IPTs)

    a. Purpose. As existing USMC diving capabilities are refined or new capabilities are developed, the proponent will establish an IPT to formally address issues arising from the Expeditionary Force Development System (EFDS) Process. Many of these issues are addressed formally through the MARCORSYSCOM Manpower & Training Plan (M&TP) Process. During this process, the IPT assesses all doctrinal, organizational, training, materiel, leadership and education, personnel and facilities (DOTMLPF) implications under the guidance of the program manager (PM). The PM uses this assessment, and any required analysis, to develop a plan for developing and sustaining the capability. The proponent's role in the IPT is to ensure that all DOTMLPF issues are addressed through facilitation and coordination of required actions, to publish all IPT findings, with all stakeholders copied, and when appropriate, to ensure and enable the participation of relevant operating forces.

    b. Membership. The proponent will include SME's from across DOD in the development of USMC diving capabilities, however IPT's formed for this purpose will consist of, at a minimum, SME representation from:

        (1) Proponent.

        (2) DC, CD&I (FMID/LID).

        (3) CG, Training Command (C461TP/AMTT).

        (4) CG, MARCORSYSCOM (IWS/R).

        (5) Commander, NAVSAFECEN (C 37), per reference (k).

4. Maritime Capability Development. USMC diving operations from newly developed maritime assets may require official authorization from the DOD diving EA. In such a case, direct involvement of the Marine Corps diving proponent is critical to effective inter-service coordination in gaining this authorization.

Chapter 3

USMC Diving Capabilities Conference

1. General. This chapter provides detailed information on the purpose, sponsorship, participants, and actions of the USMC Diving Capabilities Conference.

2. Purpose. The USMC Diving Capabilities Conference convenes annually and serves as a forum for the presentation of relevant USMC diving capability issues requiring DOD or USMC proponent action and the development of detailed Plans of Action and Milestones (POA&Ms) to resolve those issues.

3. Sponsorship. The USMC Diving Capabilities Conference is sponsored by DC, PP&O (POG). Sponsorship includes, but is not limited to, the following:

    a. Agenda Development.

    b. Administrative and Logistical Coordination.

    c. Conference Facilitation.

    d. Development of Conference Messages.

4. Participants. Units listed in chapter 4, paragraph 2a of this Order are standing members of the USMC Diving Capabilities Conference. Each of these units will send a designated diving SME to represent his command. Attending SMEs must be empowered to speak on behalf of their commanders regarding all conference agenda items. In addition to the sponsor, representation from each of the following is also required:

    a. DC, CD&I (FMID/LID).

    b. CG, Training Command (C461TP).

    c. CG, MARCORSYSCOM (PM, Reconnaissance and Amphibious Raids).

    d. Commander, NAVSAFECEN (C 37), per reference (k).

    e. Staff Noncommissioned Officer-in-Charge, Marine Combatant Diving Course.

5. Actions. At a minimum, the following actions will take place:

    a. The sponsor will establish an agenda encompassing specific issues nominated from the participants listed in paragraph 4, above, and the Operating Forces.

    b. The sponsor will facilitate the conference by ensuring that the agenda is published and followed.

    c. Attendees will receive a MARCORSYSCOM update on all current programs of record, as well as any RDT&E efforts to develop approved capabilities.

    d. Working groups will be established to address specific issues and to develop recommended courses of action as required.

e. The sponsor will develop a conference message containing the final disposition of all agenda items.

Enclosure (1)

Chapter 4

Organization

1. <u>General</u>. This chapter provides detailed information on the policy, definitions, authorities, responsibilities, and procedures associated with the organization of Marine Corps diving programs.

2. <u>Unit Types</u>. The following USMC unit types have a valid requirement to develop and maintain a viable diving capability to support prescribed missions and approved concepts of operations using equipment organic to the organization:

    a. Reconnaissance Battalions.

    b. Force Reconnaissance Companies.

    c. Training and Education Command.

    d. Marine Corps Systems Command.

    e. Marine Forces Special Operations Command (MARSOC).

    f. Marine Detachment, Naval Diving and Salvage Training Center (NDSTC).

3. <u>Diver Billets</u>. Reference (l) identifies and codifies all skill requirements for Marines. Reference (m), identifies and codifies skill and qualification requirements for Navy personnel. Authorized Marine Corps diver billets are indicated on unit Tables of Organization (T/Os) by one of the following military occupational specialties (MOS) or Navy enlisted classification (NEC) codes:

    a. 0324, Reconnaissance Man, Combatant Diver Qualified.

    b. 0326, Reconnaissance Man, Parachute and Combatant Diver Qualified.

    c. 8024, Combatant Diver.

    d. 8026, Parachutist/Combatant Diver Marine.

    e. 8403, Fleet Marine Force Reconnaissance Independent Duty Corpsman.

    f. 8427, Fleet Marine Force Reconnaissance Corpsman.

    g. 5341, Master Diver.

    h. 5342, Diver, First Class.

    i. 5343, Diver, Second Class.

    j. 8493, Dive Medical Technician.

4. <u>Table of Organization and Equipment Change Requests (TOECR)</u>. TOECRs are submitted per reference (n). All TOECRs involving diver billets or diving equipment will be forwarded to DC, PP&O (POG) for concurrence prior to approval.

Chapter 5

Administration

1. General. This chapter provides detailed information on the policy, definitions, authorities, responsibilities, and procedures associated with the administration of Marine Corps diving programs.

2. Insignia

a. Diver Insignia. Marine Corps personnel qualified as military divers are authorized to wear the diver insignia representative of the highest level of qualification, per reference (o). Those qualifications are listed below in order of precedence.

(1) Master Diver.

(2) Diver, First Class.

(3) Dive Medical Technician.

(4) Diver, Second Class.

(5) Marine Combatant Diver.

(6) SCUBA Diver.

b. Exceptions. Requests for authority to wear the Marine Combatant Diver Insignia in cases not covered above will be forwarded via the chain of command to the proponent for approval.

c. Manner of Display. Marine Corps personnel authorized to wear diver insignia will do so in compliance with reference (p) and any subsequent applicable Marine Corps bulletins in the 1020 series.

3. Assignment and Voiding of Military Occupational Specialties

a. Marine Corps personnel are assigned the corresponding diver AMOS upon successful completion of the appropriate formal course of instruction. Local administration offices will make the appropriate unit diary entries in MCTFS only after substantiating documentation is provided.

b. Requirements, procedures and authority for voiding a diver MOS are found in reference (o) and in paragraph 10 of this chapter. In addition to the requirements in the references, Marine Corps personnel may have the diver designation revoked in the event of severe safety violations or gross negligence.

4. Marine Corps Total Force System (MCTFS) Entries

a. Formal Schools. Upon successful completion and MCTIMS validation of the formal courses of instruction listed below, the corresponding Service School Code (SSC) will be entered on the education page in MCTFS.

(1) USMC Combatant Diver (N20L6H1).......................L6H.

(2) USMC Combatant Diving Supervisor (M02YH6C)..........YH6.

(3) USMC Combatant Diving Supervisor (M03YH6C)...........YH6.

(4) USMC Combatant Diving Supervisor (M10YH6C)..........YH6.

(5) USMC Combatant Diving Supervisor (M22YH6C)..........YH6.

(6) USMC Combatant Diving Supervisor (M49YH6C)..........YH6.

    b. Other Training. Formal courses of instruction still in development
or those conducted under the umbrella of new equipment training (NET) have
neither a SSC nor a MCTIMS course identification code (CID). Some examples
of such training are listed in chapter 7 of this Order. Because this
training trains and certifies Marine Corps personnel to perform specific
skills or to use specific equipment, successful completion of this training
requires official documentation. In such instances, commanders will ensure
this training is documented under the Local Schools section of the MCTFS
education page.

5. Appointments, Orders and Authorizations. Commanders will assign Marine
Corps personnel to diving duties commensurate with their billet, training and
qualifications. When required, unit special orders and/or certification
letters may serve as source documents for reporting eligibility for Diving
Duty Special Pay and applicable unit diary entries.

    a. Diving Duty. Qualified Marine Corps personnel filling valid diver
billets will be ordered to diving duty in writing. Orders may be issued
individually or collectively, however all Marine Corps personnel assigned to
diving duty will be assigned by-name to specific diver billets, and billets
will be designated by specific billet identification code (BIC) as assigned
by the Total Force Structure Management System (TFSMS). An example of diving
duty orders can be found in Figure 5-1 of this Order, however this serves as
only a guide. Commanders may issue orders to duty in the most appropriate
official format available.

    b. Command Diving Supervisor

        (1) Commanders will appoint appropriately qualified Marine Corps
personnel, Corporal and above, as command Diving Supervisors, per references
(h), (q), (r) and any additional (more stringent) unit-level diving
supervisor requirements. Qualified Marine Corps personnel will be appointed
in writing as command Diving Supervisors. An example of an appointment as a
command Diving Supervisor can be found in Figure 5-2 of this Order.

        (2) Appointment as a command Diving Supervisor applies only to diving
operations under the cognizance of the appointing commander. Command Diving
Supervisors from one unit are not authorized to perform any Diving Supervisor
duties during diving operations of another unit unless explicitly authorized
to do so in writing by the commander conducting the operation.

    c. Command Diving Officer. Commanders will appoint, in writing, an
appropriately trained, Diving Supervisor-qualified, experienced diver as the
command Diving Officer. Responsibilities and requirements for the command
Diving Officer are detailed in chapter 7, enclosure (1) of this Order. An
example of an appointment as a command Diving Officer can be found in Figure
5-3 of this Order.

d. Permissive Diving Duty

(1) Commanders of non-diving units/activities are authorized to permit previously qualified divers and diving supervisors to participate in appropriate proficiency and refresher training under permissive orders with authorized units/activities. Permissive diving duty orders will include documentation of appropriate qualification and medical clearance. An example of permissive diving duty orders can be found in Figure 5-4 of this Order.

(2) Commanders of diving units are authorized to permit appropriately qualified personnel from other units/services to participate in dive training under permissive diving orders. Commanders under whose cognizance dive operations are conducted are responsible for ensuring all participating divers and diving supervisors are qualified, current and medically cleared to participate.

6. Unit/Activity Records. Marine Corps units and activities described in chapter 4, paragraph 2a of this Order will maintain the following individual and unit documentation in accordance with reference (s).

a. Individual Records. For Marine Corps personnel within their purview, commanders will maintain all documentation pertaining to qualification, certification, recertification, assignment and/or termination as diver, diving supervisor, and/or command Diving Officer in accordance with reference (s), Standard Subject Identification Code (SSIC) 1320.1. Additionally, commanders will maintain copies of applicable permissive diving orders (with enclosures) for all personnel participating in his unit's dive operations and training on a permissive basis in accordance with reference (s), SSIC 1320.1.

b. Unit Documentation

(1) Prior to each unit dive operation, commanders will issue operations orders or letters of instruction, assigning in writing specific safety, support, and supervisory personnel for all aspects of that operation. Additionally, commanders will conduct and document an in-depth risk assessment, per reference (i). Commanders will maintain these records in accordance with reference (s), SSIC 3500.1.

(2) Following each dive operation, commanders will certify all command diving logs for that operation, using forms indicated in reference (i). Command diving logs will serve as the unit's sole source document for recording conduct of and participation in dive training and will be maintained in accordance with reference (s), SSIC 3150.2.

(3) Commanders will ensure all dives are entered into the appropriate online reporting system, as directed by the DOD diving proponent.

7. Individual Records and Logs

a. Diver Logbook. Each qualified Marine Corps combatant diver is required to maintain an individual dive log throughout his career. Logbooks will be collected by diving supervisors prior to dive operations to verify currency and determine refresher training requirements, and are returned to divers upon completion. Per reference (s), SSIC 3150.3, it is the responsibility of the diver to ensure it is updated after each dive operation, and that it remains both accurate and current. Individual diver logs may be locally produced.

b. <u>Appointments and Orders</u>. Marine Corps personnel are responsible for maintaining copies of all pertinent diving qualifications, certifications, appointments, orders and authorizations.

8. <u>Medical</u>

a. <u>Standards</u>. Medical standards for diving duty for Marine Corps personnel are prescribed in chapter 15-105, per reference (t).

b. <u>Waivers</u>. Requests to waive medical standards for diving duty listed in reference (t) will be submitted to DC, PP&O (POG) for approval via the Chief, Navy Bureau of Medicine and Surgery, Undersea Medicine & Radiation Health (M342), 2300 E. St NW, Washington, DC 20372-5300. The request will include the commander's endorsement of the medical officer's recommendation. Enclosed will be the original signed physical examination on SF-88 and personal history on SF-93. Commanders of Marines pending attendance at USMC Combatant Diver Course will send an info copy to the school for review no later than thirty (30) days prior to the class convene date. Physicals can be submitted via official mail or electronically at the addresses below:

    (1) Commanding Officer
        Attn: USMC Combatant Diver Course
        Navy Diving and Salvage Training Center
        350 South Crag Road
        Panama City, FL 32407-7016

    (2) Fax (850) 230- 5265, DSN 436-5265

    (3) Email at sncoic_mcd@navy.mil

9. <u>Unauthorized Drug Usage and Mental Instability</u>

a. Any diver (qualified or in training) charged by competent civilian or military authority with unauthorized drug usage shall be relieved of all associated duties and responsibilities and prohibited access to unit dive lockers and diving equipment. When warranted, substantiated cases may result in voiding of the diver MOS at the discretion of the proponent and MMEA-6.

b. Any diver (qualified or in training) found by competent medical authority to lack the mental stability required to function in that capacity shall also be relieved of all associated duties and responsibilities and prohibited access to unit dive lockers and diving equipment. When warranted, such cases may result in the voiding of the diver MOS at the discretion of the proponent and MMEA-6.

c. In any case where a diver is relieved for cause, all dive equipment maintained by that diver will be identified, removed from service and secured. Such equipment will undergo a thorough technical inspection prior to being placed back into service.

10. <u>Exceptions to Policy</u>

a. Requests to waive any portion of this order will be submitted via the first O-5 in the chain of command to DC, PP&O (POG) no later than forty-five (45) days prior to the related event. Electronic submissions of scanned requests and endorsements are recommended to increase effectiveness and minimize response time.

b. This Order pertains to all USMC personnel assigned to USSOCOM both individually and within MARSOC. However, in situations pertaining solely to special operations forces in the conduct of military operations, USSOCOM-specific directives may have precedence over this Order. In such instances, commanders and their divers often assume greater risk. Commanders of such units are encouraged to seek guidance from DC PP&O (POG) via their chain of command to ensure all relevant facts are understood and all potential risk is mitigated to the greatest degree possible.

c. Applicable points of contact can be found on the world-wide web at http://hqinet001.hqmc.usmc.mil/pp&o/. Replies to electronic requests will be returned in the same manner. Requests may be submitted via official mail, fax or electronically to the addresses below:

    (1) Commandant of the Marine Corps
       Headquarters United States Marine Corps
       Plans, Policies and Operations (POG)
       3000 Marine Corps Pentagon
       Washington, DC 20350-3000

    (2) Fax (703) 692-4430, DSN 222-4430

3500
Date

From: Commanding Officer
To: Sgt I.M. Marine, ###-##-1234/0321/0326 USMC

Subj: ASSIGNMENT TO DIVING DUTY

Ref: (a) MCO 3150.4
      (b) MCO P100.6G
      (c) DOD 7000.14-R, "Department of Defense Financial Management
          Regulation (FMRS)," Dates Vary by Volume
      (d) Table of Organization for UIC X#####

1. Per the references (a) through (d), you are hereby assigned to perform
diving duty effective ___date___ .

2. Your billet (BIC X#############) is coded in reference (d) for diving
duty. Per references (a) through (c), you are entitled to receive Diving
Duty Special Pay at the highest rate for which you are qualified, provided
you gain and maintain appropriate minimum qualification and currency
certifications. Failure to do so may result in the termination of diving
duty status and the forfeiture of any unauthorized payments.

3. Requirements for current and future certifications and training
progressions will be met through this or any other organization belonging to
the Department of Defense at the discretion of the individual unit commander.

4. These orders are transferable to another appropriately-coded billet in
reference (d). These orders are terminated if you are reassigned to a non-
diver billet, if you are found to no longer be qualified in the billet, upon
transfer from this command, or if otherwise revoked based on valid
justification.

5. It is certified that you are filling a billet that does not exceed the
number of billets authorized in reference (d) to receive Diving Duty Special
Pay.

                          I. M. COMMANDER

_____

FIRST ENDORSEMENT

1. Received these orders at ___command___ on ___date___ and accept them on a
voluntary basis.

                          //s//_____

                Figure 5-1.--Sample Diving Duty Orders

3500
Date

From: Commanding Officer
To: Sgt I.M. Marine, ###-##-1234/0321/0326 USMC

Subj: ASSIGNMENT AS COMMAND DIVING SUPERVISOR

Ref: (a) MCO 3150.4
      (b) U.S. Navy Diving Manual
      (c) Applicable Unit Special Orders

1. Per the references (a) through (c), you are hereby assigned as a command Diving Supervisor effective ___date___. This assignment confers my authority to you when acting as my direct representative in the function of your duties. As such, you are directly responsible to me for the safe conduct of dive operations within the scope of your duties for that operation.

2. This assignment authorizes you to perform only those diving supervisor duties for which you are appropriately qualified, and requires you to maintain appropriate minimum qualification and currency certifications as detailed in the references. Failure to do so will result in the automatic termination of this assignment.

3. This assignment terminates if you are found to no longer be qualified, upon transfer from this command, or if otherwise revoked based on valid justification.

4. This assignment is not to be considered as orders from competent authority for entitlement to Diving Duty Special Pay.

                         I. M. COMMANDER

_____

FIRST ENDORSEMENT

1. Received this assignment at ___command___ on ___date___.

                    //s//_____

          Figure 5-2.--Sample Command Diving Supervisor Assignment

3500
Date

From: Commanding Officer
To: Sgt I.M. Marine, ###-##-1234/0321/0326 USMC

Subj: ASSIGNMENT AS COMMAND DIVING OFFICER

Ref: (a) MCO 3150.4
      (b) U.S. Navy Diving Manual
      (c) Applicable Unit Special Orders

1. Per references (a) through (c), you are hereby assigned as the command Diving Officer effective ___date___. This assignment confers my authority to you when acting as my direct representative in the function of your duties. As such, you are directly responsible to me for the safe conduct of all aspects of the command's dive program per the references. Specific responsibilities as command dive officer are found in reference (a).

2. This assignment is based on your qualification and currency as a command diving supervisor and requires you to maintain appropriate minimum qualification and currency certifications as detailed in the applicable references. Failure to do so will result in the automatic termination of this assignment.

3. This assignment terminates if you are found to no longer be qualified, upon transfer from this command, or if otherwise revoked based on valid justification.

4. This assignment is not to be considered as orders from competent authority for entitlement to Diving Duty Special Pay.

                        I. M. COMMANDER

_____
FIRST ENDORSEMENT

1. Received this assignment at ___command___ on ___date___.

                  //s//_____

                Figure 5-3.--Sample Command Diving Officer Assignment

3500
Date

From: Commanding Officer
To: Sgt I.M. Marine, ###-##-1234/0321/0326 USMC

Subj: PERMISSIVE DIVE DUTY AUTHORIZATION

Ref: (a) MCO 3150.4
      (b) MCO P100.6G
      (c) DOD 7000.14-R, "Department of Defense Financial Management
          Regulation (FMRS)," Dates Vary by Volume
      (d) Table of Organization for UIC X#####

1. Per references (a) through (d), you are hereby authorized to participate
in dive training on a permissive basis, effective ___date___. This
authorization remains in effect until you are discharged, released or
transferred from this command, or you are no longer physically qualified to
participate in such activities.

2. This authorization serves as official orders, and is issued with the
understanding that your participation is voluntary, that you meet medical and
physical requirements to participate, and that your participation is at the
convenience of the command providing the support for such activities.

3. Acceptance of these permissive orders is not to be considered as orders
from competent authority for entitlement to Diving Duty Special Pay.

                         I. M. COMMANDER

_____
FIRST ENDORSEMENT

1. Received these orders at ___command___ on ___date___ and accept them on a
voluntary basis.

                         //s//_____

            Figure 5-4.--Sample Permissive Dive Duty Authorization

Chapter 6

Diving Duty Special Pay (DDSP)

1. General

    a. This chapter provides detailed information on the policy, definitions, authorities, responsibilities, and procedures associated with DDSP for USMC personnel.

    b. Requirements for diving duty pay for Marine Corps personnel are set forth in volume 7A, chapter 11 of reference (u). The following information is not all-encompassing and is provided to clarify the most common issues regarding DDSP as they are outlined in reference (u).

2. Eligibility. Marine Corps personnel who meet the criteria below are eligible to receive DDSP:

    a. Any Marine Corps personnel assigned to diving formal qualification training;

    b. Appropriately qualified Marine Corps personnel assigned to USMC T/O billets that are coded for divers who:

        (1) Are under competent orders to perform diving duty; and

        (2) Meet performance requirements as indicated in volume 7A, chapter 11 of reference (u) and paragraph 4 below.

    c. Additional requirements for DDSP for U.S. Navy personnel are established in reference (u).

3. Pay Rates. Per reference (u), DDSP for Marine Corps personnel begins at the student rate on the date of the first dive under formal instruction at an approved Armed Services diving qualification course. Upon completion of this qualification training, DDSP continues without lapse for Marine Corps personnel who are subsequently assigned to diving duty in a T/O diver billet, and DDSP increases to the standard officer or enlisted combatant diver rate.

4. Performance Requirements. Reference (u) bases a U.S. military diver's entitlement to DDSP on his maintenance of proficiency through "frequent and regular dives". The following amplifying information establishes service-wide minimum performance requirements for Marine Corps personnel to maintain diving currency and qualification for DDSP eligibility purposes.

    a. "Frequent and regular dives" are defined for Marine Corps personnel as four (4) separate dives per calendar year. Each dive must be distinct from the others, with its own dive profile (maximum depth and bottom/oxygen time). For the purposes of DDSP eligibility, each dive must be a minimum of fifteen (15) minutes in duration. Dives can be conducted at any time during the calendar year and in any environment. Dives conducted during formal dive qualification training satisfy performance requirements for a diver's first year of eligibility for DDSP. These performance requirements afford divers an entire year in which to satisfy them. Commanders are encouraged to ensure all divers within their command are afforded ample opportunity to maintain proficiency.

   b. The purpose of DDSP is to provide additional pay to increase the ability of the Marine Corps to attract and retain volunteers for diving duty, and to compensate for the more than normally dangerous character of such duty. As such, the payment of DDSP requires a diver to maintain diving proficiency. For this reason, neither surface swimming nor the performance of Diving Supervisor duties satisfies DDSP performance requirements. Commanders should in no way consider performance requirements for DDSP sufficient for the development and sustainment of a viable collective combatant diving capability. Standards for mission-related proficiency in individual and collective diving tasks and events are established in and governed by reference (w).

5. <u>Exceptions</u>. Commanders are authorized to waive performance requirements for DDSP for eligible divers who are engaged in combat operations in a hostile fire area, when a suitable training environment cannot be established. To qualify for such exemptions, divers must officially qualify for a Combat Zone Tax Exclusion, and Imminent Danger Pay must be authorized. For divers who meet this requirement, commanders may waive performance requirements for any period he deems necessary until the diver can resume training. In other cases where divers are unable to satisfy DDSP performance requirements not covered by this Order, commanders may formally request relief from these requirements from DC PP&O (POG) via the first Lieutenant Colonel or O-5 in their chain of command. Requests to waive DDSP performance requirements must provide a compelling justification to do so. Approval of such requests will be the exception vice the rule.

6. <u>Re-qualification for DDSP</u>. Any diver who fails to satisfy DDSP performance requirements for a given year becomes unqualified for DDSP on 1 January of the following year. Regardless of his assignment or billet, that diver remains unqualified for DDSP until he satisfies DDSP performance requirements in paragraph 4a above in their entirety. His DDSP begins anew on the date he satisfies the performance requirements by conducting his fourth dive. He may not receive DDSP payments for any period during which he was considered unqualified. Additionally, any unmerited payments of DDSP received during the year that the diver fails to satisfy performance requirements are subject to reclamation after-the-fact at the discretion of the first General Officer in the diver's chain of command.

7. <u>Permanent Change of Station (PCS)</u>. DDSP does not stop in instances where divers execute PCS orders from one diver billet to another. When executing PCS orders to a non-diver billet, DDSP will terminate effective the date of departure from the old duty station.

8. <u>Special Requests to Award DDSP</u>. Special requests to award DDSP to Marine Corps personnel not assigned to, or in excess of, authorized T/O billets will be forwarded via the chain of command to DC PP&O (POG) for approval. Such requests require operational necessity as a justification and each will be validated on a case-by-case basis. The most common occurrence of this requirement pertains to turnover periods between incoming and outgoing personnel filling the same diver billet. Authorization to award DDSP for Marine Corps personnel not assigned to, or in excess of, authorized T/O billets rests solely with DC, PP&O (POG).

Chapter 7

Qualification Requirements

1. Generalː. This chapter provides detailed information on the policy, definitions, authorities, responsibilities, and procedures associated with diving qualification training as it pertains to Marine Corps personnel. With the exception of USMC personnel assigned to billets within US Special Operations Command (USSOCOM), Marine Corps personnel are authorized to attend only USMC-approved formal diving-related courses of instruction, as reflected in MCTIMS, for qualification purposes. USMC personnel assigned to USSOCOM may attend DOD proponent-approved formal diving-related qualification courses as required. Prerequisites and other administrative requirements for USMC-approved courses are listed in course details in MCTIMS. Given the limited ability to verify the satisfaction of approved equipment and training standards, foreign and civilian courses of instruction are not recognized as qualification courses unless explicitly approved by DC PP&O (POG). Upon successful completion and MCTIMS validation of approved courses, appropriate entries in the Marine Corps Total Force System (MCTFS) are authorized per chapter 5 of this Order.

2. Marine Combatant Diver. The USMC Combatant Diver Course (CID N20L6H1) is the only diver qualification course approved for attendance by Marine Corps personnel. This course of instruction is taught on an individual basis and qualifies personnel to conduct underwater diving operations using Self Contained Underwater Breathing Apparatus (SCUBA) and Underwater Breathing Apparatus (UBA) Systems. Units are not authorized to transition SCUBA divers to Combatant Diver qualification. Marine Corps personnel previously qualified as SCUBA divers in a DOD diving proponent-approved SCUBA diver course may attend the closed circuit portion of Marine Corps Combatant Diver Course to complete qualification training as a Marine Combatant Diver.

3. Diving Supervisor. Reference (h) establishes the DOD proponent's requirements for Diving Supervisors. To standardize qualification requirements for the Marine Corps, CG TECOM developed the USMC Combatant Diving Supervisor Course (CID M03YH6C, M10YH6C, M22YH6C and M49YH6C) as the only USMC-approved Diving Supervisor qualification course. This course of instruction is taught on an individual basis under the cognizance of a U.S. Navy Master Diver, and it qualifies the combatant diver to serve in a supervisory role during the planning and conduct of military diving operations.

4. Command Diving Officer. The unit/activity commander will appoint, in writing, an appropriately trained and qualified diving supervisor as the Command Diving Officer. The Command Diving Officer's primary responsibility is the safe conduct of all diving operations within the command. The Command Diving Officer will become thoroughly familiar with all command diving techniques and will have a detailed knowledge of all applicable regulations and a rudimentary understanding of reference (x) and the Navy Maintenance and Material Management (3-M) system. He is responsible to the commander for all operational and administrative duties associated with the command diving program. Detachments of more than thirty (30) days duration intending to exercise a diving capability must also have an assigned Diving Officer. With the exception of detachments of short duration, appointments will be for no less than six (6) months.

5. <u>Prior Service Qualifications</u>. Marine Corps personnel with prior service, regardless of branch, are subject to the requirements in this Order. Qualifications as a diver and/or diving supervisor via any other means than those authorized in this Order are invalid. Prior service personnel who cannot meet the qualification requirements in this Order are considered unqualified and require formal training. Exceptions to this policy are authorized by the USMC diving proponent only.

6. <u>New Equipment Qualification Training</u>. Due to the high risk, equipment-centric nature of military diving, divers and diving supervisors are qualified to perform their respective duties using only that equipment that they are qualified to use. Prior to using other new diving equipment, divers will receive appropriate training per published equipment-specific training plans. In the absence of such service-wide directives, unit Master Divers will dictate training requirements for divers and diving supervisors on this equipment.

Chapter 8

Formal Training Requirements and School Seat Management

1. <u>General</u>. This chapter provides detailed information on the policy, definitions, authorities, responsibilities, and procedures associated with formal dive training requirements and school seat management for Marine Corps personnel.

2. <u>Formal Training Requirements</u>

    a. Marine Corps seats to DOD diving courses are used exclusively to train Marine Corps personnel assigned to authorized billets, or in receipt of official orders to such billets. Authorized billets are defined in chapter 4 of this Order.

    b. Training requirements for units identified in chapter 4 of this Order are presented to and validated by CG, TECOM, Formal Schools Training Branch (C4611) via the Training Input Plan (TIP) process per reference (e). DC, PP&O (POG) will validate and prioritize requirements for military diving courses as requested by CG, TECOM (C4611).

3. <u>Formal Training Allocations</u>. Seats to formal diving courses of instruction are allocated by CG, TECOM (C4611) to major commands and occupational field sponsors (OFS) based on operational necessity. Major commands and OFSs with allocated seats are encouraged to coordinate one-for-one exchanges of assigned seats in order to resolve scheduling conflicts caused by operational and deployment tempo, and are required to report all exchanges to CG TECOM (C4611) for inclusion into the Training Quota Memorandum (TQM) via a TQM change.

4. <u>Unprogrammed Requirements and Late Requests</u>

    a. <u>Unprogrammed Requirements</u>. Allocated seats are intended to fill stated and validated requirements only, however urgent and/or unique operational requirements may merit exception to policy. Requests for exception to this policy will be submitted via the chain of command to DC, PP&O (POG) per chapter 5 of this Order, and each will be considered on a case-by-case basis. These requests are both unbudgeted and unprogrammed, are not eligible for funding by the Worldwide TAD (WWTAD) Fund and require unit TAD funding to execute.

    b. <u>Late Requests</u>. Requests to attend diving courses of instruction submitted later than ten (10) working days prior to the published report date are considered late requests. Late requests are not eligible for funding by the Worldwide TAD (WWTAD) Fund and require unit TAD funding to execute.

5. <u>Vacant Formal School Seats</u>

    a. Seats to any diving courses that remain unfilled fifty (50) days prior to the published report date will be recouped by DC, PP&O (POG) for reclassification and reallocation via MCTIMS.

    b. On occasion, seats to diving courses may become available due to late cancellations. When solicited by DC, PP&O (POG), commanders of units and personnel meeting the criteria specified in chapter 4 of this Order are encouraged to use these seats provided that unit TAD funds are used and all Marine Corps funded and programmed seats are filled.

6. Formal School Attendance in a Permissive Temporary Additional Duty (PTAD) Status. Marine Corps personnel are not authorized to attend formal diver qualification courses of instruction while in a Permissive TAD status, and must be ordered to diving duty by competent authority.

Chapter 9

Proficiency and Refresher Training

1. General. This chapter provides detailed information on the policy, definitions, authorities, responsibilities, and procedures associated with dive proficiency and refresher training for Marine Corps personnel.

2. Limitations on Proficiency Training. Only DOD personnel who successfully complete DOD Proponent-approved diving courses of instruction may participate in Marine Corps diving operations or training, and participation is limited to the duties and type of operation and equipment for which the individual is qualified. USMC civilian employees and contractors with job/position descriptions including diving duty must have formally trained and qualified at an approved U.S. military diving school as either a USMC combatant diver, scuba diver, Second Class diver, or First Class diver. Marine Corps civilian divers are governed by the provisions of references (h) and (q), this Order, and U.S. Government Occupational Safety and Health Administration (OSHA) diving standards, delineated in reference (y).

3. Requirements for Proficiency and Refresher Training. While commanders of U.S. Navy diving units rely heavily on their Master Divers to advise them on diver proficiency, few USMC commanders have such an asset. Because diving skills are perishable and require periodic sustainment training to maintain proficiency, the USMC diving proponent establishes the minimum currency requirements for qualified Marine Corps divers and diving supervisors. Currency requirements may not be relaxed under any circumstance, and applies to all Marine Corps personnel regardless of status, qualification or billet. Refresher training is a matter of safety and a function of ORM. As always, commanders may impose more stringent requirements within their purview. This training requirement has no bearing on eligibility for DDSP. Currency requirements for US Navy personnel are established in and governed by reference (v).

    a. Divers. Divers with less than six (6) months of elapsed time since their last dive are considered current. Divers whose currency expires must complete unit-sponsored dive refresher training prior to diving again. This training will be conducted under the cognizance of a qualified and current diving supervisor, and at a minimum it will focus on the skills, tasks and equipment relevant to the next dive.

    b. Diving Supervisors. USMC Diving Supervisors with less than six (6) months of elapsed time since supervising their last dive (whether alone or under instruction) are considered current. Diving Supervisors whose currency expires must complete Diving Supervisor refresher training prior to supervising their next dive. This training will include supervision under instruction, will be conducted under the cognizance of a qualified and current diving supervisor, and must be approved by the command Diving Officer.

4. Responsibilities.

    a. Divers. When manifesting for Marine Corps dive operations, divers are required to inform the diving supervisor if that dive will be their first dive following either initial qualification training or any 6-month lapse in proficiency training with the equipment planned for the upcoming dive.

b. <u>Diving Supervisors</u>. While divers are required to inform the diving supervisor as detailed in the previous paragraph, it is the responsibility of the diving supervisor to ensure that all divers are both qualified and current to conduct the operation using the equipment planned.

5. <u>Permissive Dive Training</u>

a. <u>Purpose</u>. Commanders of units without a diving capability are encouraged to afford qualified Marine Corps divers the opportunity to maintain currency and qualification when feasible. Likewise, commanders of units with a diving capability are also encouraged to afford qualified Marine Corps divers the opportunity to participate in unit training when practical. When authorized by their commander to participate in dive operations and training on a permissive basis, all proficiency and refresher training requirements apply, including any additional requirements of the host unit.

b. <u>Requirements for Participation</u>. Participation of Marine Corps personnel in Marine Corps dive operations and training on a permissive basis may be conditionally authorized by the commander of the unit conducting the operations. Criteria for such participation are as follows:

(1) An appropriate qualification course, as detailed in this Order, has been successfully completed by each participant and validated by the commander of the unit conducting the dive operations/training.

(2) Participants possess written authorization to participate in such operations/training on a permissive and not-to-interfere basis from their own operational commander per chapter 4 of this Order.

(3) Participants are medically qualified to participate in the specific type of dive operations, per reference (t).

(4) After conducting an in-depth operational risk assessment, the commander of the unit conducting the dive operations determines that such participation presents minimal and acceptable risk to all participants.

Chapter 10

Unit Training and Operational Requirements

1. <u>General</u>. This chapter provides detailed information on the policy, definitions, authorities, responsibilities, and procedures associated with unit requirements pertaining to dive training.

2. <u>Debriefs</u>. Diving Supervisors will conduct a detailed after-action debrief prior to the conclusion of each dive operation. This debrief will cover the observations, lessons-learned and recommendations for future operations of all key personnel and participants.

3. <u>Medical Support</u>. General medical support required for diving operations is detailed in reference (h). Additional requirements are defined below.

    a. <u>Personnel</u>. Medical support personnel for Marine Corps dive operations will be assigned no other duties for the operation which they support. In the event that assigned medical support personnel are required to leave the dive site, closed circuit oxygen diving operations will cease until medical support requirements are satisfied.

    b. <u>Recompression Chambers</u>. With the exception of 'No Decompression Dives', recompression facilities within six (6) hours of transit time are required for the conduct of peacetime diving operations. For dive operations during emergencies, deployments, or combat operations, these requirements may be satisfied by portable systems. Per the Diving Supervisor checklist, it is mandatory that a civilian or military dive chamber is identified and contacted before commencing any diving operations.

4. <u>Sleep and Medication</u>. Dive operations are high-risk operations. Risk level and the probability of mishaps increase when divers and Diving Supervisors do not get sufficient rest. Therefore, commanders will ensure that all divers and key support personnel are afforded adequate rest prior to dive operations and training as a function of ORM. No personnel directly involved with dive operations shall consume alcohol within 12 hours of dive operations. All medications used by divers must be approved and the diver cleared by a Special Amphibious Reconnaissance Corpsman, Dive Medical Technician, or Dive Medical Officer. The use of drugs affecting the safe conduct of dive operations is strictly prohibited.

5. <u>Participation of Marine Corps Personnel with Other Services and Agencies</u>. Following an in-depth risk assessment, unit commanders and officers-in-charge may authorize qualified and current Marine Corps personnel in their charge to participate in diving operations conducted by other U.S. military services or agencies.

6. <u>Participation of Marine Corps Personnel with Foreign Military Services</u>. Per reference (q), participation in diving operations with foreign military services is limited to personnel assigned to the DOD personnel exchange program (PEP). All other diving requires Navy approved and/or certified equipment, systems and procedures. Exceptions from this policy require prior approval from CNO (N773) via DC PP&O (POG).

7. <u>Participation of Non-Marine Corps Personnel in Marine Corps Dive Operations</u>. Following an in-depth risk assessment, Marine Corps unit commanders and officers-in-charge may authorize participation of other

appropriately qualified DOD uniformed personnel, U.S. Government civilian employees, MARCORSYSCOM-approved contractors, MCCDC-approved contractors, MEF/DIV-approved life support maintenance technician contractors, and foreign military personnel in Marine Corps dive operations. Upon meeting all criteria for participation in permissive dive operations per chapter 9 of this Order, such personnel may be authorized in writing to participate in Marine Corps dive operations by the first O-5 in the chain of command of the unit conducting the dive operations.

8. <u>Combat Operations</u>

a. Authority to waive safety policy and/or prescribed operating procedures for diving during combat operations rests with the first General Officer in the chain of command. In situations where gaining General Officer approval may jeopardize mission success, the first Lieutenant Colonel or O-5 in the chain of command may authorize specific deviations from established policy or procedure.

b. For all instances of waiving or deviating from established policy or procedure, DC, PP&O (POG) will be officially notified via Naval Message as soon as possible.

Chapter 11

Diving Equipment

1. General. This chapter provides detailed information on the policy, definitions, authorities, responsibilities, and procedures associated with dive equipment.

2. Authorized Users and Maintainers

    a. Only Marine Corps units and activities with an authorized allowance of dive equipment on their Table of Equipment (T/E) are authorized to possess and maintain dive equipment or to conduct dive operations.

    b. Marine Corps units and activities with authorized diver billets, but lacking equipment allowances, may be supported on a not-to-interfere basis, based on operational mission requirements, by the nearest appropriate Marine Corps unit or activity possessing the appropriate equipment.

3. Authorized Equipment. Only equipment found in reference (z) and in appropriate Marine Corps stock lists is authorized for use by Marine Corps personnel in military diving.

4. Restrictions and Limitations on Use of Equipment

    a. Government-Owned Equipment. Government-owned diving equipment will be used for approved military operations only and will not be used for off-duty activities.

    b. Personally-Owned Equipment. The use of personally-owned diving life support equipment (tanks, regulators, buoyancy systems, etc.) during Marine Corps dive operations is prohibited.

5. Diving Equipment Maintenance Requirements

    a. Only qualified and current divers are authorized to pre-dive, post-dive, maintain, and store diving life support equipment per technical manuals for that specific equipment. Maintenance of diving equipment will be conducted per references (h) and (x).

    b. At a minimum, two appropriately qualified divers are required to pre-dive and post-dive life support diving equipment- one to work, and one to inspect. This requirement applies to all units, in garrison and deployed.

6. Alteration of Diving Equipment. Alteration of approved diving equipment is strictly prohibited without prior written approval by CG MARCORSYSCOM (IWS/R).

7. Defective Equipment. Defective equipment will be reported, per references (h) and (aa), using the Failure Analysis Reporting process at https://secure.supsalv.org/faradd.asp.

8. Dive Lockers

    a. Inspections. Per reference (k), the Naval Safety Center, Norfolk, VA will conduct MCCDC funded inspections of each diving locker annually for units without a Master Diver and every 2 years for units with a Master Diver.

Representatives from the unit/activity's command, DC, PP&O (POG), and/or MARCORSYSCOM (IWS/R) may accompany the survey team as required. It is the responsibility of the unit commander to adhere to survey results and correct deficiencies per the survey team's recommendations. Repeat discrepancies from the previous inspection and trends will be reported by the Naval Safety Center to DC, PP&O (POG), and/or MARCORSYSCOM (IWS/R).

   b. <u>References</u>. Requirements for the maintenance, operation and accountability of USMC dive lockers are governed by both references (h) and (aa).

Chapter 12

Reporting Requirements

1. <u>General</u>. This chapter provides detailed information on the policy, definitions, authorities, responsibilities, and procedures associated with reporting requirements pertaining to dive training.

2. <u>Equipment Malfunctions and Incidents</u>. Commanders will report all dive equipment malfunctions of dive equipment, per references (h) and (aa). An equipment malfunction is defined as the failure of the system or piece of equipment to perform as originally designed whether the equipment failed, human error, or emergency procedure was required. This includes, but is not limited to equipment failures resulting in buoyancy control activation, sodasorb failure, unusual dry suit leakage, DPD throttle malfunction, or sudden loss of oxygen pressure.

3. <u>Responsibility</u>. While the responsibility to report all malfunctions and incidents, per references (h) and (aa), ultimately rests with the unit commander or officer-in-charge, timely compliance with report requirements is a shared duty between the diving officer, diving supervisor, and divers, as well as the unit Master Diver and medical department.

4. <u>Accidents Involving Injury or Death</u>. In addition to requirements outlined in references (f) and (h), official Naval Message notification of diving malfunctions and incidents resulting in injury or death will be submitted within 24 hours of the incident by the individual's parent command to each of the plain language address designators (PLADs) below.

   a. CMC WASHINGTON DC PPO POG.

   b. CMC WASHINGTON DC MRA MR MRC.

   c. CG MARCORSYSCOM IWS.

   d. COMNAVSAFECEN.

5. <u>Suspected Malfunction of Equipment</u>. In addition to requirements outlined in references (f) and (h), official Naval Message notification of suspected malfunction of dive equipment will be submitted within 12 hours of the malfunction via the chain of command to each of the PLADs below. In the event that access to a Naval Message handling system is unavailable, a telephonic report can be submitted as a last resort.

   a. CMC WASHINGTON DC PPO POG.

   b. CMC WASHINGTON DC SD.

   c. CG MARCORSYSCOM IWS.

   d. CG MARCORSYSCOM MC2I.

   e. COMNAVSAFECEN.